FAITH HILL
THE HITS

MW00779710

SPECIAL THANKS TO:

JULIAN PEPLOE
Art Direction / Package Design

Alfred Publishing Co., Inc.
16320 Roscoe Blvd., Suite 100
P.O. Box 10003
Van Nuys, CA 91410-0003
alfred.com

ISBN-10: 1-7390-5087-7
ISBN-13: 978-1-7390-5087-3

CONTENTS

6

RED UMBRELLA

Words and Music by
AIMEE MAYO, CHRIS LINDSEY,
BRETT WARREN and BRAD WARREN

8

Verse 2:
You can wear your sorrow like an old raincoat,
You can save your tears in a bottle made of gold.
But the glitter on the sidewalk always shines,
Yeah, even God needs to cry sometimes.

Pre-chorus 2:
Your love is like a red umbrella,
Always there to make me better.
When my broken dreams
Are fallin' from the sky.
(To Chorus:)

STRONGER

(Live)

Music and Lyrics by
HILLARY LINDSEY and TROY VERGES

14

Stronger - 6 - 3
29187

I_____ just want us to be free.

Ba-by, I'm sor-ry for the way___ things are. Good-bye is al-ways hard.___

But we both will___ be strong___ er.___

Verse 3:
I can't believe you're really gone,
But I know it's for the best.
Baby, I know that we weren't right,
I still reach for you each night,
And, man, it hurts like hell.
So, cry for me, baby...
(To Chorus:)

LOST

Words and Music by
KARA DIOGUARDI and MITCH ALLAN

21

Lost - 7 - 4
29187

24

CRY

Words and Music by
ANGIE APARO

30

Cry - 7 - 2
29187

32

Bridge:

Give it up, ba - by,___ I hear you're_ do - ing fine.___

Noth-ing's gon - na save me___ 'til I see it in your eyes.

Cry - 7 - 4
29187

cry_____ a lit - tle for me?

Verse 2:
If your love could be caged, honey,
I would hold the key
And conceal it underneath the pile of lies you handed me.
And you'd hunt those lies,
They'd be all you'd ever find.
And that'd be all you'd have to know for me to be fine.

Chorus 2:
And you'd cry a little,
Die just a little.
And, baby, I would feel just a little less pain.
I gave, now I'm wanting
Something in return.
So cry just a little for me.
(To Bridge:)

MISSISSIPPI GIRL

Words and Music by
JOHN RICH and
ADAM SHOENFELD

From Touchstone Pictures' PEARL HARBOR

THERE YOU'LL BE

Words and Music by
DIANE WARREN

43

There You'll Be - 5 - 2
29187

44

45

There You'll Be - 5 - 4
29187

THE SECRET OF LIFE

Words and Music by
GRETCHEN PETERS

The Secret of Life - 7 - 1
29187

Verse 3:

3. Sam looks up from his Sun-day pa - per, says, "Boys, you're on___ the wrong

track. The se-cret of life is, there ain't no se - cret

and you don't___ get your mon - ey back." ___ Hey,___ the se-cret of life___ is___ get -

Chorus:

Repeat ad lib. and fade

Verse 2:
You and me, we're just a couple of zeros.
Just a couple of down-and-outs.
But movie stars and football heroes,
What have they got to be unhappy about?
So they turn to the bartender,
"Sam, what do you think?
What's the key that unlocks that door?"
Sam don't say nothin',
Just wipes off the bar
And he pours them a couple more.

Chorus 2:
'Cause the secret of life is in Sam's martinis.
The secret of life is in Marilyn's eyes.
The secret of life is in Monday Night Football,
Rolling Stones records, and mom's apple pies.
(To Verse 3:)

THE WAY YOU LOVE ME

Words and Music by
KEITH FOLLESE and
MICHAEL DELANEY

BREATHE

Words and Music by
HOLLY LAMAR and
STEPHANIE BENTLEY

Verse 1:

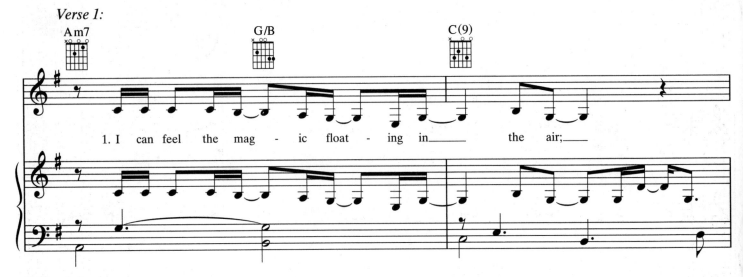

1. I can feel the mag - ic float - ing in___ the air;___

Breathe - 6 - 1
29187

62

Breathe - 6 - 5
29187

LET ME LET GO

Words and Music by
DENNIS MORGAN and STEVE DIAMOND

*Original recording down 1/2 step in F#.

Let Me Let Go - 6 - 1
29187

66

THIS KISS

Words and Music by
ROBIN LERNER, ANNIE ROBOFF
and BETH NIELSEN CHAPMAN

71

This Kiss - 4 - 2
29187

72

IT MATTERS TO ME

Words and Music by
ED HILL and MARK D. SANDERS

Gtr. tuned down 1/2 step:
⑥ = E♭   ③ = G♭
⑤ = A♭   ② = B♭
④ = D♭   ① = E♭

Slowly (♩ = 66)

(with pedal)

Verse:

1. Ba - by, tell me where'd you ev - er learn___ to
2. *See additional lyrics*

It Matters to Me - 5 - 1
29187

78

Verse 2:
Maybe I still don't understand
The distance between a woman and a man.
Tell me how far it is,
And how you can love like this.
I'm not sure I can.
(To Chorus:)

WILD ONE

Words and Music by
JAIME KYLE, PAT BUNCH
and WILL RAMBEAUX

80

PIECE OF MY HEART

Words and Music by
BERT BERNS and JERRY RAGAVOY

88

Repeat ad lib. and fade

Verse 2:
You're out on the street lookin' good, baby.
Deep down in your heart you know that it ain't right.
No, you'll never hear me cryin', you know I cry all the time.
Each time I tell myself that I can't stand the pain.
You hold me in your arms and I start singin' once again.
So come on, come on, come on and...
(To Chorus:)

I NEED YOU

Music and Lyrics by
DAVID LEE and TONY LANE

Fa-ther and the Son__ need the Ho - ly Ghost,__

I need you.__

Oh,_____ I_____ need you.__

Verse 3:

(Tim:) 3. I wan - na drink that shot of whis -